Ernest Hemingway, Cub Reporter

Williams
Tucker
Moorhead
Raull

Hemingway

Moorhead
Hemingway
Jackson
Smith
Dickey
Williams
Smith

Wilson
Jackson

Smith

Moorhead
Fitz-Jack
Vaughn
Tucker
Jackson
Smith

Fitz
Hicks
Williams—Fitz
Hicks
Alford
Hemingway
Mooney
Wallace
Mooney
Hicks
Wilson
Tucker
Wilson
Mrs Powell
Smith
Moorhead
Hemingway
Hinkle
Williams
Hemingway

Courts
Prosecutor's office
City Hall
Police Headquarters
Station No.4 and Bo   side Court
Fires
Coroner
Undertakers
Hospitals
General Hospital
Municipal Court
Union Station
Commercial Club
Federal Bldg
Hotels
Justices
Schools and Library
Politics
Weather
Banks
Real Estate
Metropolitan
River, etc..
City Hall annex Wilson, Gillette
Inside Alford, Soldier Mooney
Inside Gillette, Raull, Godfrey.
Gambling Controversy
Raids go on—One Commissioner may remain.
Bond Campaign
Cool—Cudahy can store how much?
Street Car service committee asleep
Conductoresses' classes
School inspection
Gas and Strike
Draft
Aviation—recruiting
Income taxes
War Work—Need More Knitters again
Grand Jury story
Dr. Tiffany—St Lukes
Capt John Pellatier dead-picture
Breweries
Firemen
Kansas City War Community Service. 311 Victor Bldg.
Will Huttig, Jr. —picture
Smallpox Hospital
Louise Kirk—suicide, Hoppe, Wiseman
Symphony Orchestra Campaign today for $12,000
U.S.Labor Agencies
Hold six Italians
Take G?hours Sons Shot.
Ellwood Cut Lines
Salary fund transfers
Hemingway his cards

ckey Railroad interlock

Call Pruec on Rotary Club.

Normal Cadets x ★

4 30 Grand ave Teup
WH Allen on ta...
Discussion

MEN
Jackson
Moorhead
Higgins (RR)
Marsh
Godfrey
Ormiston (RR)
Alford
Williams
Dickey
Hicks
Wilson
Collins
Tucker
Fitz
Hemingway
Wallace.
Smith.
Vaughn.
Raull.
Mooney.
Gillette.

The *Kansas City Star* assignment sheet for 3 January 1918 showing Hemingway's daily routine

ERNEST HEMINGWAY, CUB REPORTER

Kansas
City
Star
Stories

Edited by
MATTHEW J. BRUCCOLI

University of
Pittsburgh Press

ISBN 0–8229–3193–1
Library of Congress Catalog Card Number 73–101189
Copyright © 1970, University of Pittsburgh Press

Acknowledgments for illustrations:
Assignment sheet reproduced by the courtesy of the Monroe County
Public Library, Key West, Florida
"Battle of Raid Squads" photograph from the collection of C. E. Frazer
Clark, Jr., used by permission
Kansas City Star style sheet reproduced by the courtesy of the Beinecke
Library, Yale University

To Aurora

It is the height of silliness to go into newspaper stuff I have written, which has nothing to do with the other writing which is entirely apart and starts with the first In Our Time. *Have written thousands of columns in newspapers. Also sent much in condensed cable-ese to be rewritten in U.S. and Canada. This has nothing to do with signed and published writing in books or magazines and it is a hell of a trick on a man to dig it up and confuse the matter of judging the work he has published. If anyone wants to do that after a man is dead, he can't defend himself, but while he is alive, he can, at least, take no part in it and oppose it as far as possible. The first right that a man writing has is the choice of what he will publish. If you have made your living as a newspaperman, learning your trade, writing against deadlines, writing to make stuff timely rather than permanent, no one has the right to dig this stuff up and use it against the stuff you have written to write the best you can.*

Ernest Hemingway in Louis Henry Cohn,
A Bibliography of the Works of Ernest Hemingway, 1931

I am violating Hemingway's instructions because he now belongs to history, and every bit of his writing matters. The key ideas in the letter to Captain Cohn are that in his early reporting Hemingway was learning his trade and that it is wrong for anyone to use this apprenticeship journalism "against" his major work. This may have been true in 1931, but now there is no question of hurting his reputation. Now every fact helps us to understand his career; and, in particular, Hemingway's apprenticeship can provide special insights. It is always instructive to observe a giant in the process of becoming a giant.

M.J.B.

Contents

Preface

> On the *Star* you were forced to learn to write a
> simple declarative sentence. That's useful to any-
> one.
>
>> Ernest Hemingway,
>> *The Paris Review*, Spring 1958

CHARLES FENTON'S *The Apprenticeship of Ernest Hemingway* (New York: Farrar, Straus, 1954) demonstrates
the importance of Hemingway's seven-month stint on the
Kansas City Star (1 October 1917–30 April 1918) in
shaping the style and material of his fiction. Fenton argues
that the *Star*'s style sheet (first rules: "Use short sentences.
Use short first paragraphs. Use vigorous English. Be posi-
tive, not negative.") influenced the economy, accuracy,
and force of the great Hemingway style. And Hemingway
acknowledged the usefulness of this training. In a 1940
interview he recalled the staff's concern for clear writing:
"Those were the best rules I ever learned for the business
of writing. I've never forgotten them. No man with any
talent, who feels and writes truly about the thing he is trying to say, can fail to write well if he abides with them"
("Back to His First Field," *Kansas City Times*, 26 November 1940, 1).

Hemingway's favorite assignment, the short-stop run—
the railroad terminal, the general hospital, and police station number four—exposed him to violence and death.
He drew upon this Kansas City material in vignettes for
in our time (1924):

At two o'clock in the morning two Hungarians got into a cigar store at Fifteenth Street and Grand Avenue.

They hanged Sam Cardenella at six o'clock in the morning in the corridor of the county jail.

And in "God Rest You Merry Gentlemen" (1933):

In those days the distances were all very different, the dirt blew off the hills that now have been cut down, and Kansas City was very like Constantinople.

The usefulness of Fenton's study was limited by his inability to identify Hemingway's *Star* work, none of which was by-lined. Only one story is discussed by Fenton, "Mix War, Art and Dancing" (21 April 1918), a sad sketch which Hemingway wrote with controlled sentiment and economy of prose about a whore excluded from a fashionable dance.

It is now possible to attribute with some confidence eleven *Star* stories to Hemingway. Although they are certainly not a representative sampling—most of Hemingway's work for the *Star* was the routine assignments given to cub reporters, as shown by the assignment sheet—the best of these stories show an interest in the objective description of violence and a desire to reveal character through speech and action. The *Star* work also suggests one reason why Hemingway did not return to full-time reporting after World War I. Perhaps—in addition to his ambition to write fiction—routine coverage of the hospitals, undertakers, and railroad station simply did not interest him. The compulsion to be where things were happening and to find out for himself what was really going on is manifest in the best of Hemingway's apprentice journalism. The hospital vignettes in "At the End of the Ambulance Run" (20 January 1918) and "Kerensky, the Fighting Flea" (16 December 1917), which are still readable, show that Hemingway—like another reporter-novelist, Stephen Crane—was more interested in color stories and character sketches than in straight reporting.

The texts of the newspaper stories have been transcribed exactly as they originally appeared. No silent emendations have been made.

I thank my research assistants, Elizabeth Wells and Jennifer Atkinson. I acknowledge the permission to reprint these stories granted by Cruise Palmer, Executive Editor of the *Kansas City Star*; and I thank Mrs. Betty M. Bruce of the Monroe County Public Library, Key West, Florida, for providing the *Kansas City Star* assignment sheet. The "Battle of the Raid Squads" was reprinted in the December 1968 issue of *Esquire Magazine* accompanied by the editor's headnote in slightly different form.

My debt is great to C. E. Frazer Clark, Jr., for the freedom of his Hemingway collection and for his constant collaboration.

With Hemingway Before *A Farewell to Arms*

With Hemingway Before
A Farewell to Arms

Theodore Brumback

THERE WAS something queer about the typewriter the tall, dark-haired chap at the next desk was pounding. Every tenth letter or so would print above the type line. He didn't seem to mind. Nor did he mind when two keys would jam. They seemed to do this more frequently as he warmed to his subject.

On my fourth trip to the water cooler for a drink I stopped behind him to watch. It was my first day as a cub reporter on *The Kansas City Star*. The city editor had forgotten my existence. I had nothing to do but drink water and hit myself on the kneecap to see whether my leg would jump or not.

When the tall chap had finished his story he called for a copy boy. Then he turned to me.

"That's rotten looking copy," he said with a smile. "When I get a little excited this damn type mill goes haywire on me. Sometimes I can't even read what I've written. The copy reader may call me over to the desk in a minute to translate. They kid me a lot, but they print my stuff just the same."

"Your thoughts are faster than your fingers."

"Something like that." He arose and came towards me with outstretched hand. "My name's Hemingway—Ernest Hemingway. You're a new man, aren't you?"

That was my introduction to the man who has since

3

become one of our greatest contemporary writers. I wish I could pat myself on the back and say that I recognized his ability even then. But I didn't. Not until later. My first impression of him was that of a big, handsome kid, bubbling over with energy. And this energy was really remarkable. He could turn out more copy than any two reporters. He never seemed to be tired at the end of the day.

One Saturday night after we had finished work, Hemingway suggested that I spend the night with him. In those days reporters didn't have motor cars. So we boarded an owl car for the section of the city where Hemingway had what he called his "lodgings." These lodgings consisted of a tiny, dismal room in the attic of an old-fashioned frame house in an unfashionable part of the city. It was a long ride there and I was almost asleep when we got to his room.

"Like poetry?" Hemingway demanded suddenly. The pajamas hung in folds on me. I was inches shorter than their owner.

"Sure, some kinds."

"Let's read a little Browning out loud."

"At this time of night? Are you crazy?" It was after 1 and I was dead.

"Aw, come on. I have a jug of dago red here that'll make a new man of you. What do you say? We'll only read for a half hour or so."

"Well—" It was pretty hard to refuse the man anything, especially when he turned on that smile. He had gotten the wine and was pouring out some for me. I took my glass and lay on the floor with a pillow under my head.

4

Hemingway began to read in a clear, penetrating voice. He read well and I enjoyed it until I began to doze. He wouldn't let me do that for long, however.

"Here," he said, "you read a while. My voice's getting husky."

I did my best but I'm no Browning interpreter. After a little I got the effect as if I were reading in a foreign tongue, unknown to me. It was weird to read page after page without understanding a word.

Hemingway saw how things were and took the book away from me. I tried to listen to him read, but after a poem or so I was asleep.

A crick in my neck woke me. I looked at my watch. It was 4 o'clock. Hemingway was still reading.

"For the love of Mike, Ernie," I said, "You must be nuts."

He smiled. And that smile you'd have to see to appreciate. It broke out all over his face, revealing a deep dimple in his cheek. He looked as fresh as a daisy.

"Sure I'm nuts," he answered. "But what's the dif? I knew you'd gone to sleep. I like to read out loud. I get the flavor of the poetry better. So I just kept at it. I thought you'd wake up once in a while and take a little of it in. But you didn't."

The next day he got through his work as if nothing had happened. Sometimes I think that's the outstanding characteristic of genius—boundless energy. When the rest of us mortals have finished our work we're ready for play or bed. But your genius has only started.

Most of the "leg men," as reporters who worked on the outside were called, had regular runs. Each day they stopped at places which were steady sources of news. Occasionally they would be given special assignments. Hemingway's run included the General hospital and the union station. They were always good for short features or news stories.

Until the union station massacre, which was to happen many years later (he would have given much to have been present, I'm sure) Hemingway wrote one of the most important stories to originate from that source. It happened this way.

One day, when he was making his rounds, he noticed a crowd collected in a corner of the rotunda of the station. On the stone floor lay a man on a stretcher. He was bundled in blankets. The crowd had formed a circle around him at a respectful distance, for his face was broken out in ugly sores. There seemed to be no one attending him. He was moaning a little.

"What's the trouble here?" Hemingway demanded.

"He's got a contagious disease," someone in the crowd replied. "No one dares touch him. Some one sent for an ambulance."

"Why is he left alone like this? Isn't anyone in charge of him?"

"Two men took him off the train and brought him here. Then they went back to the train. I suppose the man's a pauper and couldn't afford to pay anyone to take care of him."

"How long since they sent for the ambulance?"

"About half an hour."

Hemingway swore. "Why, I wouldn't treat a dog like that. What's the matter with you people? Why didn't some of you carry him out on the stretcher and put him in a taxi and send him to the General hospital? The man's got smallpox and will die if not given care immediately. I know what smallpox is because I'm a doctor's son and recognize the symptoms. Who'll help me get him out of here?"

At the word smallpox, the crowd retreated. No one offered to help. Hemingway became angry. "What's the matter with you yellow bunch anyway? Are you going to stand there and let a man die?"

When still no one made a move, he himself picked up the man in strong arms and carried him out of the station. Then he ordered a taxicab and took him personally to the General hospital, charging the expense to The Star.

In March of that year, 1918, we got a chance to go to war. Hemingway was delirious with excitement. We were to leave in June with a Red Cross ambulance unit for Italy, Italy of all places.

"Well, I'm no slacker now," he said the day we received our notice. He referred to a sore subject. On account of a slight defect in sight he had been turned down for the American army. This preyed upon his mind and made him morose at times. The war fever was hard to resist in those days.

We went over on no American transport convoyed by destroyers.

The venerable Chicago of the French line braved the submarine zone alone. We were on deck the night she sailed without lights. There had been reports of a U-boat operating along the American coast and Hemingway was delighted. But nothing came of it.

The Chicago was a great disappointment. The only excitement was lifeboat drill. Then we discovered there were more people than there were places in the lifeboats.

"What's the dif?" Hemingway said, patting his ancient life preserver. "We've got as good a chance as those in the boats. They might get shelled, anyway."

I didn't feel that way. I preferred a place in the boat. But there was nothing to do about it. The French officers merely shrugged their shoulders. The nurses were first, weren't they? And then the very estimable Y.M.C.A.

The monotony of the trip made us forget our fears. There was nothing to do but play poker in the bar, where a game went on day and night, or shoot craps. Here you had to be a quick thinker, for you were apt to be "covered" in French, English, Belgian, Italian, or American money. Hemingway tried it but found he was behind, although he'd won. There was no way to beat it.

The barman was an angular Frenchman with a walrus mustache who spoke English with a cockney accent. He interested Hemingway. At the first life boat drill he brought him on deck, protesting, where he was photographed with us. The barman had no use for the drills. Neither did we after the first one.

The day we reached the submarine zone there was great excitement. A barrel on a raft was sighted. The commander of the Chicago changed his course. The gossip was that it was a German trap. There was a submarine about that would torpedo us if we stopped to find out what the raft meant. We never learned the truth nor did we ever see a submarine. Hemingway felt he'd been cheated.

When we arrived in Paris the Germans were shelling

the capital with their long range guns, news of which had startled the world. The number of casualties from the shells were surprisingly small, considering that some landed in crowded streets. After the first surprise and fright, the Parisian populace went about its business as usual. Some of the more timid remained inside during the shelling. The Germans had failed in their purpose, which was to shatter French morale.

As I said, the day we arrived shelling was going on. Hemingway was as excited as if he'd been sent on special assignment to cover the biggest story of the year. As we left the Gare du Nord we could hear the bursts from different parts of the city.

"Come on, Ted," he said. "We're going to see something. Here taxi."

One of those 2-cylinder affairs that saved Paris at the first battle of the Marne chugged up to us. We got in with our suitcases and other luggage.

"Tell him to drive us to where those shells are falling," Hemingway commanded. "We'll get a story for The Star that'll make their eyes pop out back in Kansas City."

I was nervous. "Listen, Ernie, don't you think we'd better use a little discretion? There's no sense in deliberately exposing ourselves to danger. How would this look in The Star: 'Two Kansas Citizens were killed today while sightseeing in Paris?' "

He smiled. "Why there's no chance of us getting bumped off. Out of the millions of people in Paris how many get killed by shells? You can count 'em on the fingers of your hand."

"That all might be so," I replied, "but you don't see

any Parisians chasing around just to see where the shells burst, do you? Any Frenchman would think you insane if you told him what you wanted to do. And I'll bet that, if I can make our driver understand what we want, he'll refuse to drive us."

"Well, all right. If you don't want to go, I'll go by myself."

Now what are you going to do with a man like that?

"OK," I said. "Let's go."

When I finally made our driver understand where we wanted to go, he became blasphemous. I thought he was going to have a stroke of apoplexy. I couldn't understand a word he said out of the torrents he hurled at me. But I knew what he meant. He was saying no.

"Offer him more money," Hemingway said.

I held up a franc note of good sized denomination. The torrent of blasphemy stopped at once. The little driver bowed and scraped, *"Mais, certainment, messieurs."*

So we started on one of the strangest taxi rides I shall probably ever experience. The German long range gun, being quite a distance from Paris—seventy-five miles, I believe—the enemy could not expect to hit any particular part of the capital. They shot at the city in general. Consequently the shells burst in various widely separated areas.

Well, believe it or not, we spent an hour or so chasing over the city before we finally caught up with a burst. The shell hit the facade of the Madeleine, chipping off a foot or so of stone. No one was hurt. We heard the projectile rush overhead. It sounded as if it were going to land right in the taxi with us. It was quite exciting. After that the Germans signed off for the day.

I've forgotten now whether Hemingway wrote a story about our taxi adventure. I never saw it. But if he did it must have been pretty good. That sort of subject was right up his alley. [Brumback's article continues with an account of Hemingway's experiences in Italy.]

Kansas City Star
6 December 1936

The *Kansas City Star* Stories

Kerensky, the Fighting Flea

16 December 1917, 3C

Attributed to Hemingway by D.H. [Donald Hoffman] who cited in the *Kansas City Star* (28 January 1968, 1D) the recollections of Neil McDermott, a *Star* office boy in Hemingway's time. Reprinted by Mel Foor ("Remembering Hemingway's Kansas City Days," *Kansas City Star*, 21 July 1968, 1D–2D).

Somehow, although he is the smallest office boy around the place, none of the other lads pick on him. Scuffling and fighting almost has ceased since Kerensky came to work. That's only one of the nicknames of Leo Kobreen, and was assigned to him because of a considerable facial resemblance to the perpetually fleeing Russian statesman, and, too, because both wore quite formal standing collars.

In size, Leo is about right for spanking. But that never will happen to Leo. Although he is inches short of five feet, there is a bulkiness about his shoulders that gains respect even from those Cossacks of the business world, the messenger boys.

In fact, it was a messenger, coming in blusteringly, who first made it known that

15

Leo possessed a reputation. Almost politely the cocky young fellow handed a yellow envelope to the office bantam.

"Why it's Kid Williams," he said. "Are you going to fight at the club Saturday night, Kid?"

"I should have known it," the boss said. "Kerensky has all the characteristics of a prize fighter. After a short round of work doesn't he retire to a corner and sit down?"

Then some of them remembered Kid Williams in preliminary bouts . . . One of those boys who scrap three rounds before the big fighters enter the ring. That's Kerensky.

You may have thrown some loose change into the ring at the final gong. How you laughed to see the two bantams push each other about and scramble fiercely each to pick up the most. Sometimes they couldn't wait to get their gloves off. All the fight fans roared at them trying to pick up thin dimes in their padded fists.

"That's all hippodrome stuff," Kerensky says. "The men like to see us quarrel over the money, but win or lose, we split it fifty-fifty. My half of the pickup runs from $1.50 to $2.50."

The worst thing about the fight game, take it from Kerensky, is the smoke. He has even considered retiring from the ring because it is so upsetting to take a deep breath of tobacco fumes.

"But of course I haven't quit," he explains. "Right now if I knew some of the clubs downtown had a smoker on and they offered me $2, of course I'd get in and fight."

How would Kerensky advise a young man to open a pugilistic career? Well, he just picked up his skill. For several years he sold papers, and you know how one thing leads to another. There is a newsboy rule that if one boy installs himself on a corner no other can sell there. A full grown man used to cry the headlines on a certain Grand Avenue crossing. Poachers bothered him.

"It wouldn't look right for a big fellow to hit a little kid," says Kerensky, "so he let me sell there, too, and sicked me on all the strange boys. I always ran them away. He liked me and called me Kid Williams, after the bantamweight champion."

Kerensky's last street fight was to a big gate. A newsboy of larger growth was the victim. They clinched and fell to the sidewalk. A crowd gathered, but the crossing patrolman turned his back till the battle was over. Then he came over and said: "Leo, I guess you'll have to cut this out."

After that, when Leo wanted to fight, somebody had to hire a hall. He began going into the gymnasiums to sell papers. There he watched the big men train for their Convention Hall bouts. Sometimes the proprietors would let him come in and work out beside Thorpe or Chavez for nothing. It costs the ordinary citizen a dime, Leo says, to get in and work at the pulleys and weights at times like these.

His opportunity came to go on in a newsboy bout at a smoker in Cutler's gymnasium. The kid glows yet at the mention of that bout.

"It was the best fight of my career," he says. "I went in mad, and gave the fans their money's worth. But I was awful green, and was almost knocked out in the last round. Now I know how to study 'em, and I don't have to work as hard."

After hard days in old Russia, the life is full of joy for Leo, and who can say that he is not making the most of his opportunities? When he talks of the past it is of a pogram. That Christmas season the workmen in a sugar refinery near Kiev made a cross of ice and set it up on the frozen river. It fell over and they blamed the Jews. Then the workmen rioted, breaking into stores and smashing windows. Leo and his family hid on the roof for three days, and his sister fell ill of pneumonia. One studies to change the subject and asks:

"Leo, do they ever match you with a bigger boy?"

"Oh no," he says, "the crowd wouldn't stand for that. But sometimes I catch one on the street."

Battle of Raid Squads

6 January 1918, 1

Reprinted with my headnote in *Esquire* (LXX [December 1968], 207, 265). Dr. Clarence E. Hemingway retained a clipping of the story with this note: "Ernest's work entire colun" (collection of C. E. Frazer Clark, Jr.). Hemingway recalled the story in 1940: "Ernest Hemingway stood in his cowman's boots in a room at the Hotel Muehlebach last night, the rain beating against the east windows, remembering the Kansas City of twenty-odd years ago—how Southwest Boulevard slanted and how he lay under a Ford while detectives shot two internal revenue agents . . ." ("Back to His First Field," *Kansas City Times*, 26 November 1940, 1).

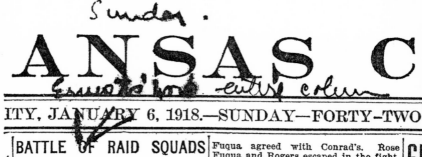

Clipping which Hemingway sent to his father, Dr. Clarence E. Hemingway, as a sample of his journalistic work. The note is Dr. Hemingway's.

20

Foor's *Star* article ("Remembering Hemingway's Kansas City Days," 21 July 1968) noted this interview and stated that "research shows no such occurrence." In a letter to *Esquire* (LXXI [February 1969], 12), Foor explained: "After several interviews, particularly with the *Star*'s police reporter in 1918, Bill Moorhead, I came to the conclusion that Hemingway did not cover this story. Moorhead claims that Hemingway worked the police beat for only one week in March, 1918, and otherwise was not directly involved in police reporting. He said E.H. did not cover this story. I might add that The *Star* would not assign a cub—more so then than now—to cover a story of this importance, and his only chance to have been there would have been just that—chance." Nevertheless Hemingway said he was there and proudly sent a clipping of the story to his father.

The story may have been phoned in.

> John M. Tully and Albert Raithel, revenue officers from St. Louis, may die, and two city detectives narrowly escaped injury as a result of a revolver battle yesterday through a case of mistaken identity. Tully and Raithel had gone to raid a house at 2743 Mercier Street, reported to be a rendezvous for drug users. Edward Kritser and Paul Conrad, city detectives, arrived a few minutes later on the same mission. Each party of officers mistook the other for drug peddlers.

Tully was shot in the right leg, left arm and lower abdomen. Raithel was wounded in the abdomen and left wrist. Both will recover. The two detectives were uninjured, but both had bullet holes through their clothing.

The wounded men were taken to the General Hospital. Later they were removed to the Swedish Hospital.

While on the surface the shooting of the two government officers appeared to be a case of mistaken identity, elements of a mysterious nature which Francis M. Wilson, United States district attorney, refused to make public, crept into the case last night.

At 11 o'clock last night the district attorney took a statement from Tully. He said he could not disclose its contents. It was admitted by another government official there was "something back of the whole affair."

It was said all of the evidence with regard to the shooting and developments leading to the affair will be placed before Hunt C. Moore, prosecutor. Senator Wilson said the government would co-operate with the prosecutor. The district attorney conferred two hours last night with Chief Flahive and John Halpin, police commissioner. At the close Senator Wilson said he felt certain the prosecuting attorney would do his duty in the case.

Tully gave this story of the shooting:

"Raithel and I received information that there was a nest of drug addicts at a house at 2743 Mercier Street. We secured a search warrant from S.O. Hargis, assistant United States district attorney, and went out. In the house was an old woman. We questioned her and could learn nothing, so left to watch the house and question a few of the neighbors. We were standing across the street when a motor car drove up and two men and a girl got out. One of the men carried a handbag. Raithel and I thought they were 'dope heads.' I went to the front door and Raithel to the rear. Inside the door I saw Bernie Lamar's girl. She said, 'Hello Jack.' Then a man stepped out of the next room. I walked up to him and touched him on the shoulder, saying, 'Hold on a minute, I'm an officer.' Then he started shooting. He got me in the arm. I shot twice and then got out the door. I got across the street and fell in front of a house. Then the other man shot me again. I emptied my revolver and then staggered over to a garage across the road."

Raithel was operated on as soon as he was taken to the hospital and was unable to make a statement.

The two detectives told a different story. According to them the battle was the culmination of a fued between a gang of drug addicts and government agents.

About seven months ago Bernard Aberer, a notorious police character was sent to the Fort Leavenworth prison for drug peddling. John Tully had secured the evidence that convicted Aberer. His wife, Rose Aberer, alias Rose Fuqua, known as Rose Lamar, has been living here with a man named William "Irish" Rogers, also a drug addict and holder of a police record. When Tully arrested Aberer the government secured a large quantity of narcotics. Lately the federal officials here have been trailing Rose Fuqua, trying to locate the rest of the big supply of drugs which she was believed to have hidden. Two special agents were sent from the St. Louis office to aid in the work.

Friday night Rose Fuqua and Williams were shadowed to the Stratford Hotel, 616 East Eighth Street, where they registered as Mr. and Mrs. William Sullivan. Yesterday the revenue office obtained two detectives from police headquarters to aid in raiding the room at the Stratford. Kritser and Conrad were assigned. Rose, a man named Richard C. Adams, and Rogers were arrested in the room and a quantity of narcotics found. The woman confessed to the government agents that the missing drugs were hidden in her mother's home at 2743 Mercier Street. The city detectives took her and Rodgers out to the address.

Conrad and Kritzer found a sack containing a quantity of heroin, morphine, opium and two complete "hop smoking" outfits hidden in the house. Conrad says he was talking to Rose Fuqua in the front room of the 5-room frame house when he heard a knock on the door. A man entered. The woman said, "Hello, Jack, how are you?" Conrad said in a sworn statement.

"I concluded from the familiar way he spoke to her that he was a member of the gang," the detective said. "The man turned to me and said 'Who are you?' reached for his revolver and reached for my shoulder. I drew my revolver and fired twice. He shot at me three times. One bullet went through my coat, another grazed the side of my face. My shot struck him and he reeled out of the front door. Another man (Raithel) shot at me through the window. I fired three times and then went behind a door to reload my gun.

"I heard someone shooting in the rear of the house and saw Kritser shooting at a man across the street. I stepped around and exchanged shots with a man shooting from behind a grocery wagon. I thought we were fighting a gang of dope fiends and rushed to the next house on the north, firing as I went. Kritser and I both shot at a man firing across the street. The small man dropped. Someone yelled, 'They're government men.' We stopped firing. Neither one of them said anything about being officers to me."

Kritser's story and that told by Rose Fuqua agreed with Conrad's. Rose Fuqua and Rogers escaped in the fight, but later gave themselves up.

Buddie, a dog owned by Rogers, was shot in the leg and is being taken care of by a neighbor. Adams, Rogers, and Rose Fuqua are being held at police headquarters for investigation.

At the End of the Ambulance Run

20 January 1918, 7C

Attributed to Hemingway by Foor ("Remembering Hemingway's Kansas City Days," *Kansas City Star*, 21 July 1968). These vignettes have clear connections with the vignettes of *in our time* (1924) and the Kansas City hospital story, "God Rest You Merry Gentlemen" (1933). The Negro who refuses to identify his assailant anticipates Cayetano of "The Gambler, the Nun, and the Radio" (1933). In addition to the violent material, other characteristics of Hemingway's later work are to be seen in these vignettes: the unsentimental tone, the presentation of character through speech, and the use of detail.

The night ambulance attendants shuffled down the long, dark corridors at the General Hospital with an inert burden on the stretcher. They turned in at the receiving ward and lifted the unconscious man to the operating table. His hands were calloused and he was unkempt and ragged, a victim of a street brawl near the city market. No one knew who he was, but a receipt, bearing the name of George Anderson, for $10 paid on a home out in a little Nebraska town served to identify him.

The surgeon opened the swollen eyelids. The eyes were turned to the left. "A fracture on the left side of the skull," he said to the attendants who stood about the table. "Well, George, you're not going to finish paying for that home of yours."

"George" merely lifted a hand as though groping for something. Attendants hurriedly caught hold of him to keep him from rolling from the table. But he scratched his face in a tired, resigned way that seemed almost ridiculous, and placed his hand again at his side. Four hours later he died.

It was merely one of the many cases that come to the city dispensary from night to night—and from day to day for that matter; but the night shift, perhaps, has a wider range of the life and death tragedy —and even comedy, of the city. When "George" comes in on the soiled, bloody stretcher and the rags are stripped off and his naked, broken body lies on the white table in the glare of the surgeon's light, and he dangles on a little thread of life, while the physicians struggle grimly, it is all in the night's work, whether the thread snaps or whether it holds so that George can fight on and work and play.

Here comes another case. This time a small man limps in, supported by an ambulance man and a big policeman in uniform. "Yes, sir, we got a real robber this time—a real one—just look at him!" the big officer smiled. "He tried to hold up a drug store, and the clerks slipped one over on him. It was a—"

"Yes, but they was three of 'em, an' they was shootin' all at once," the prisoner explained. Since there was no use in attempting to deny the attempted robbery, he felt justified in offering an alibi for his frustrated prowess. "It looks like I oughtta got one of 'em, but then, maybe, I'll do better next time.

"Say, you'd better hurry up and get these clothes off of me, before they get all bloody. I don't want 'em spoiled." He was thoroughly defeated and dejected, and the red handkerchief he used for a mask still hung from his neck.

He rolled a cigarette, and as the attendants removed his clothes, a ball of lead rattled to the floor. "Whee! It went clear through, didn't it? Say, I'll be out before long, won't I, doc?"

"Yes—out of the hospital," the physician replied significantly.

Out on Twenty-seventh street a drug clerk—the one of the three who used the .38—has a .38 bullet dangling from his watch chain.

One night they brought in a negro who had been cut with a razor. It is not a mere joke about negroes using the razor—they really do it. The lower end of the man's heart had been cut away and there was not much hope for him. Surgeons informed his relatives of the one chance that remained, and it was a very slim one. They took some stitches in his heart and the next day he had improved sufficiently to be seen by a police sergeant.

"It was just a friend of mine, boss," the negro replied weakly to questioning. The sergeant threatened and cajoled, but the negro would not tell who cut him. "Well, just stay there and die, then," the officer turned away exasperated.

But the negro did not die. He was out in a few weeks, and the police finally learned who his assailant was. He was found dead—his vitals opened by a razor.

"It's razor wounds in the African belt and slugging in the wet block. In Little Italy they prefer the sawed-off shotgun.

We can almost tell what part of the city a man is from just by seeing how they did him up," one of the hospital attendants commented.

But it is not all violence and sudden death that comes to the attention of the emergency physicians. They attend the injuries and ills of charity patients. Here is a laborer who burned his foot one morning when he used too much kerosene in building the fire, and over there is a small boy brought in by his mother, who explains there is something the matter with his nose. An instrument is inserted into the nostril of the squirming youngster and is drawn forth. A grain of corn, just sprouted, dangles at the end of the steel.

One day an aged printer, his hand swollen from blood poisoning, came in. Lead from the type metal had entered a small scratch. The surgeon told him they would have to amputate his left thumb.

"Why, doc? You don't mean it do you? Why, that'd be worse'n sawing the periscope off of a submarine! I've just gotta have that thumb. I'm an old-time swift. I could set my six galleys a day in my time —that was before the linotypes came in. Even now, they need my business, for some of the finest work is done by hand.

And you go and take that finger away from me and—well, it'd be mighty interesting to know how I'd ever hold a 'stick' in my hand again. Why, doc!—"

With face drawn, and head bowed, he limped out the doorway. The French artist who vowed to commit suicide if he lost his right hand in battle, might have understood the struggle the old man had alone in the darkness. Later that night the printer returned. He was very drunk.

"Just take the damn works, doc, take the whole damn works," he wept.

At one time a man from out in Kansas, a fairly likable and respectable sort of man, to look at him, went on a little debauch when he came to Kansas City. It was just a little incident that the folks in the home town would never learn about. The ambulance brought him from a wine room, dead from a stroke of heart disease. At another time (it happens quite often) a young girl took poison. The physicians who saved her life seldom speak of the case. It she had died her story might have been told—but she has to live.

And so the work goes on. For one man it means a clean bed and prescriptions with whisky in it, possibly, and for another, it is a place in the potters' field. The skill of the surgeon is exercised just the same, no matter what the cause of the injury or the deserts of the patient.

———————————

The telephone bell is ringing again. "Yes, this the receiving ward," says the desk attendant. "No. 4 Police Station, you say? A shooting scrape? All right, they'll be right over." And the big car speeds down the Cherry Street hill, the headlights boring a yellow funnel into the darkness.

Throng at Smallpox Case

18 February 1918, 3

There are differences between Brumback's account of this story (see pp. 6–7) and the actual story.

> While the chauffeur and male nurse on the city ambulance devoted to the carrying of smallpox cases drove from the General Hospital to the municipal garage on the North Side today to have engine trouble "fixed" a man, his face and hands covered with smallpox pustules, lay in one of the entrances to the Union Station. One hour and fifteen minutes after having been given the call the chauffeur and nurse reported at the hospital with the man, G.T. Brewer, 926 West Forty-second Street. The ambulance had been repaired.
>
> Behind that vehicle was an ambulance from the Emergency Hospital, ordered to get the patient by Dr. James Tyree, in charge of contagious diseases, after repeated calls from the station.
>
> Brewer, a life insurance agent, arrived from Cherryvale, Kas., this morning. At 9 o'clock James McManus, officer in charge of the police station at the depot,

found him lying in the west entrance to the lobby. Streams of persons, hurrying past, eddied about Brewer while solicitous passersby asked the trouble. At 9:50 McManus placed a policeman near the sick man to keep persons away.

McManus says he called the contagious department of the hospital immediately after finding Brewer. An ambulance was promised. Two calls were sent the hospital later and each time, so McManus says, he was told the ambulance was on the way. Doctor Tyree once insisted McManus take the sick man into the police office there, but McManus refused, saying more persons would be exposed. Doctor Tyree also said the ambulance would be there "right away."

When the ambulance did reach the station, at 10:15, the driver explained it had been broken down while out on another call.

Doctor Tyree explained later that the regular sick ambulance, No. 90, was wrecked last night. When the call first was received at the receiving ward of the General Hospital at 9:05 o'clock ambulance No. 92, the smallpox carrier, was dispatched, he said.

"But the ambulance had motor trouble," Doctor Tyree continued. "The chauffeur and the male nurse in charge decided to go to the municipal garage and get the trouble fixed."

The garage, on the North Side, is about as far from the hospital as the distance from the hospital to the Union Station and return.

Doctor Tyree criticized the police for failure to remove Brewer to an isolated place instead of leaving him "where scores of travelers came in contact and were exposed to smallpox."

Laundry Car Over Cliff

6 March 1918, 1

Background on this story is provided by Foor ("Remembering Hemingway's Kansas City Days," *Kansas City Star*, 21 July 1968). Hemingway was sent on this assignment with an older reporter, William B. Moorhead, who remembers that Hemingway antagonized the mob of strikers by identifying a rock thrower to the police. The story was phoned in.

Laundry strike sympathizers drove a Walker Laundry Company motor truck over Cliff Drive hill at Hardesty Avenue late this afternoon, after capturing the car and routing the driver and two special officers at Fourteenth Street and Euclid Avenue. One of the special officers fired a shot into the crowd before fleeing from the rain of bricks and stones. No one was injured.

Homer Maze, 5106 East Twenty-fourth Street, was driving the laundry truck. Guarding him were two special officers, Sam Seaman, 2700 East Twenty-seventh Street, and C. L. Winner, 717 East Eleventh Street.

Maze was making a delivery at Fourteenth Street and Euclid Avenue when a crowd of about twenty-five men and women approached from the west and opened fire of rocks and stones on the standing car. Maze came from the house and made a run to join the special officers. After several minutes of fusillading stones, the officers and Maze deserted the car and reported the disturbance at the Flora Avenue Police Station. Seaman, one of the special officers, told of firing a shot toward the crowd, attempting to disburse the strike sympathizers. Re-enforcements joining the attacking party seemed to arrive steadily, they said, so they gave up the car to the crowd.

When the police arrived at the scene of the disturbance a part of the crowd was yet there. Six men and one woman were arrested. The men could not be identified by Maze or the special officers as having thrown stones. The woman, Julia Anderson, 1711 West Prospect Place, was identified by them and was held on a $51 cash bond. She denies having thrown anything.

The truck was found after a search, but is practically demolished.

A second "wrecking party" was reported from Eleventh Street and Chestnut Avenue. B. L. Ferguson, 6424 Lee Street, driver of a Kansas City Laundry Com-

pany truck, and a special officer, Salvator Schira, 1911 Missouri Avenue, were attacked by fifteen men and twelve women. A stone thrown by one of the striking laundry workers struck Ferguson on the cheek, another on the right hand. His injuries are not severe.

Six Men Become Tankers
17 April 1918, 7

Big Day for Navy Drive
17 April 1918, 6

Navy Desk Jobs to Go
18 April 1918, 17

Would "Treat 'Em Rough"
18 April 1918, 4

Recruits for the Tanks
18 April 1918, 6

Dare Devil Joins Tanks
21 April 1918, 3A

Hemingway sent clippings for the first five of these recruiting stories to his family as samples of his work, noting that he had been writing the stories about the army, navy, marines, and British-Canadian and tank services (19 April 1918; collection of C. E. Frazer Clark, Jr.). It is possible that "Dare Devil Joins Tanks" was also by Hemingway.

Six Men Become Tankers

Six men were accepted today for the new tank corps by Lieut. Frank E. Cooter, who arrived from Washington yesterday to recruit men for the special service. The men were selected from a crowd of twenty that appeared at the army recruiting office at Twelfth Street and Grand Avenue today. Men of various occupations, from bookkeepers to motor operators, applied for service today. Those accepted are:

Elvin L. Loyd, 1711 Penn Street, a tractor driver.

Harold E. McEachron, Atlanta, Ga., a machinist.

Kenneth C. Dills, 3939 Agnes Avenue, stenographer.

Robert E. Watson, 1317 West Thirteenth Street, stenographer.

Albert F. Henne, 207 East Twelfth Street.

Lewis M. Dean, Chicago, Ill.

The men of the tank corps enlist in a dangerous branch of the service, but it is thrilling work and, like aviation, has long periods of rest and inactivity between the short, concentrated spells of action.

All the men taken were of draft age and were given a letter from Col. I. C. Welborn of the tank corps, authorizing any local board to immediately induct them into service.

A returned officer from the western front now training recruits at the national tank training camp at Gettysburg, Pa., tells the inside story of one of the land ships in action.

For several days the men prepare for the coming offensive. The tanks are brought up behind the first line trenches under cover of darkness and the crews crawl into the close, oily smelling steel shells. The machine gunners, artillerymen and engineers get into their cramped quarters, the commander crawls into his seat, the engines clatter and pound and the great steel monster clanks lumberingly forward. The commander is the brains and the eyes of the tank. He sits crouched close under the fore turret and has a view of the jumbled terrain of the battle field through a narrow slit. The engineer is the heart of the machine, for he changes the tank from a mere protection into a living, moving fighter.

The constant noise is the big thing in a tank attack. The Germans have no difficulty seeing the big machine as it wallows forward over the mud and a constant stream of machine gun bullets plays on the armour, seeking any crevice. The machine gun bullets do no harm except to cut the camouflage paint from the sides.

The tank lurches forward, climbs up, and then slides gently down like an otter on an ice slide. The guns are roaring inside and the machine guns making a steady typewriter clatter. Inside the tank the atmosphere becomes intolerable for want of fresh air and reeks with the smell of burnt oil, gas fumes, engine exhaust and gunpowder.

The crew inside work the guns while the constant clatter of bullets on the armour sounds like rain on a tin roof. Shells are bursting close to the tank, and a direct hit rocks the monster. But the tank hesitates only a moment and lumbers on. Barb wire is crunched, trenches crossed and machine gun parapets smothered into the mud.

Then a whistle blows, the rear door of the tank is opened and the men, covered with grease, their faces black with the smoke of the guns, crowd out of the narrow opening to cheer as the brown waves of the infantry sweep past. Then it is back to barracks and rest.

"We want fighters for the tank service," said Lieutenant Cooter today. "Real men that want to see action. No mollycoddles need apply." Men from 18 to 40 years old are being enlisted at the army recruiting station, Twelfth Street and Grand Avenue. Men of nearly all mechanical trades may enlist if they pass the personal inspection and mental test given by Lieutenant Cooter.

Big Day for Navy Drive

The second day of the naval drive for recruits for immediate duty took sixty-one
men into the recruiting office at Eighth
and Walnut streets. Thirty-eight were accepted, the largest number enlisted any
day this year. Men enlisted were of all
ratings, seventeen seamen, five firemen,
two radio men, two hospital apprentices,
five carpenter's mates and three painter's
mates.

Carpenters and painters are offered
special inducements to enroll in the Naval
Reserve under the new pay schedule. Both
are enlisted in three classes, first, second
and third class carpenter's mates. Artisans
must have at least three years' experience
in their trades before they may qualify for
any of the ratings. A third class carpenter's mate receives $41 a month, second
class $46 and first class $52. Carpenters
are given a separation allowance, clothing allowance, subsistence allowance and
medical attention without extra charge.

Lieut. Ralph B. Campbell, in charge of
the recruiting here, has compiled figures
to show a third class carpenter, the lowest
paid rating, receives the equivalent of
$150 a month. Reservists now are being

sent to the Great Lakes Training Station as fast as they are enlisted. Fifty left last night. Radio reserve men are under command of Commandant Moffett of Great Lakes and are being called alphabetically. The letter S was reached in the call today.

Navy Desk Jobs to Go

There will be no more desk warriors of draft age in the naval reserve as soon as an order issued by the bureau of navigation this morning goes into effect. By the order, all naval reservists of draft age who have had six months' training are at once ordered to sea duty unless they are physically disqualified. Reservists on recruiting duty, holding publicity jobs, doing any inland work, must leave at once for sea service.

Eight men will be lost from the naval recruiting station at Eighth and Walnut streets by the new order, Lieut. Ralph Campbell, head of naval recruiting here, said today.

Marguerite Clark, motion picture idol, who recently enrolled as a yeowoman in the naval reserve, will not be affected by the order, Lieutenant Campbell said, as it has not yet been extended to women.

The Great Lakes station has been called on to furnish a quota of six men a week to be sent to the engineer officers' section of the officers' material school at Pelham Bay Park, N.Y. Men enrolling in the reserve now will have a chance to qualify for the technical instruction at Pelham Bay.

Men completing the course are commissioned ensigns and made junior deck officers.

Men now taking a course in technical school may enroll in the reserve to be sent to the Pelham Bay school on the completion of their college work. Eight students from the Kansas State Agricultural College arrived here today to enroll in the reserve for officers material. Four are in the junior class and four in the senior.

The seniors will go to the school on graduation. The juniors will be given a chance to qualify at this summer vacation.

Four men stood outside the army recruiting office at Twelfth Street and Grand Avenue at 7:45 o'clock this morning when the sergeant opened up. A stout, red faced man wearing a khaki shirt was the first up the stairs.

"I'm the treat 'em rough man," he bawled. "That cat in the poster has nothing on me. Where do you join the tankers?"

"Have to wait for Lieutenant Cooter," said the sergeant. "He decides whether you'll treat 'em rough or not."

The fat man waited outside the door. By 9 o'clock thirty men crowded the third floor hallway. The stout man was nearest the door. Just behind him was a gray haired man wearing a derby, a well cut gray suit, a purple tie, socks to match and a silk handkerchief with a light purple border peeping from his vest pocket.

"I'm over draft age and it doesn't matter what my profession is," he said. "I never really wanted to get into this war before, but the tanks are different. I guess I can treat 'em rough."

The crowd grew steadily. By 10 o'clock there were forty applicants. Some of the men were humming, others talking among themselves. The stout man, perspiration pouring down his face, held his place next the door. He tried to whistle, but his lips wouldn't pucker. He stood on one foot, then the other. He mopped his face with a handkerchief, and finally bolted out through the crowd.

"He looked pretty hot, but he got cold feet," a mechanic in overalls commented.

After the fat man left there was a slight exodus. A high school boy with a geometry book decided in favor of school. Two flashily dressed youths said, "Aw, let's get a beer." One man, saying nothing, slipped away.

"Can't stand the gaff," said the mechanic.

But most of the applicants stayed. A youth wearing an army shirt explained: "It's my girl. I belonged to the home guards and she kind of kidded me. Nobody's going to kid a tanker, I guess."

The opinion of most of the men was voiced by a clerk. "I don't know anything about tractors or machinery, but I can learn to work a machine gun and I want to get across. Gee, I hope I get in."

A little man with double lens glasses said: "I don't suppose they'll take me. Guess I'm pretty useless. But I want to try. It's about my last chance. They all throw me down."

When Lieut. Frank E. Cooter, special tank recruiting officer, appeared, the crowd formed a line outside the door. The men were admitted one at a time. Moistening their lips, they entered the little room and stated their qualifications.

John R. Ecklund, 27 years old, was one of the first admitted. "What mechanical experience have you had?" he was asked. "None. I'm an attorney for the Kansas City Street Railways Company," he replied.

"Why do you want to join?"

"I want to see action and get over in a hurry."

Lieutenant Cooter accepted him.

"That is the type of all of them," the lieutenant said. "That is what brings men here. Not promises of high pay or easy service, but telling the truth about quick action and danger. 'To know and yet to dare,' would be a good slogan. Quick service, quick promotion and action, action, is what brings them. They are the finest type of men for soldiers.

Besides Ecklund six other men were accepted for service up to noon.

Recruits for the Tanks

A line of men wound from the front room of the third floor of the Army recruiting station, Twelfth and Grand Avenue, through the hall and half way downstairs. Some of the men were jostling and laughing, others looked sober and looked thoughtfully at the posters on the wall. Mechanics in overalls, bookkeepers, stenographers, school teachers who would have difficulty with the physical examination, and athletic college students, all were in line.

The head of the line stopped at the door of a room where a freckled faced young second lieutenant sat at a desk. He nodded, a man was admitted, asked a few questions, sized up by the lieutenant and then either told he was not wanted or given a card to sign.

"It's the spirit of adventure which brings them up here," said Lieut. Frank E. Cooter, of the Tank Corps, the latest branch of the United States Army. "Every man in line there is a potential crusader. They may not have realized it until today. Then they came up to enlist. We do not offer anything easy. The tank corps is no place for those that want noncombatant jobs and desk soldiers needn't apply. But we guarantee quick action, active service, a good chance for a commission and adventure. The tank work is dangerous, of course, but men will always apply for clean, dangerous work with a chance for quick advancement."

More than fifty men applied at the recruiting office yesterday and Lieutenant Cooter recommended the enlistment of eighteen. Men of mechanical skill are wanted especially but an order from Col. I. C. Welborn, of the tank corps authorized Lieutenant Cooter to accept any men "qualified by soldierly qualities."

Arthur McKnight and Albert Findley, Kansas City newspapermen, enlisted in the new service yesterday. The other men enlisted ranged in occupation from truck drivers to school teachers. Letters and telegrams of application were received from all over the Middle West yesterday.

Dare Devil Joins Tanks

"Have you ever had any gas engine experience?" asked Lieut. Frank E. Cooter, special tank officer at the army recruiting station, Twelfth Street and Grand Avenue, yesterday.

"Well, you might call it that," replied William A. Whitman, 914 East Ninth Street. "I've driven a Blitzen-Benz at the Chicago, New York, Cincinnati and Los Angeles speedways for the last four years. You might call my race with Ralph Mulford at Reno a gas engine experience. Or the time the old boat got up to 111 miles an hour at the Sheepshead Bay track, or when Bob Burman was killed on the big board oval and I piled up right behind him. Those were gas engine experiences."

"But have you had any military experience?" asked Lieutenant Cooter.

"Well, not regular military. I held a lieutenant's commission in the Nicaraugan army in the war against Honduras in 1909. I was also a machine gun captain with Madero when he put Diaz out. First American to get into Juarez. Ask Pancho Villa, he knows. But none of those were very military. I had a commission in a couple of Central American revolutions, too. Nothing very military there, either."

Lieutenant Cooter shoved a blank toward him. "Sign on the dotted line, man," he said. "You're too good to be true!"

"Well, I haven't raced since September at Sheepshead Bay, and I may be a little out of practice, but you don't have to go so fast in a tank. Besides, I've got a little difficulty with my teeth. But I sure want to sign for the tanks."

Lieutenant Cooter has wired Washington requesting waivers as to the teeth.

Besides the regular quota of mechanics, barbers, motor car salesmen, bartenders and college students who applied yesterday, Maynard Bush, 38 years old, instructor in journalism at Polytechnic Junior College, made out an application. He will not be enlisted until next week, so he may arrange for a successor.

Letters were received from several Kansas University students who wish to enter. The Sigma Alpha Epsilon Chapter at Manhattan, Kas., wrote that several of its members wished to enlist. Telegrams and letters came throughout yesterday in regard to the tank service.

One hundred and sixteen men were accepted by Lieutenant Cooter during the week for immediate service. Nineteen were taken yesterday.

Mix War, Art and Dancing

21 April 1918, 1

Fenton comments that Hemingway won congratulations from his associates for this story: "Hemingway received the accolade several times, in particular for a story which he himself remembered, many years later, as 'very sad, about a whore.' . . . Hemingway's exposition was wholly implicit; he avoided both sentimentality and cheapness. The treatment was instinctive anticipation of one of the strengths of his later work. The story impressed George Longan, the city editor, as much as it did [C. G.] Wellington. There were enthusiastic prophecies about the eighteen-year-old boy's journalistic future" (*The Apprenticeship of Ernest Hemingway*, p. 46).

Outside a woman walked along the wet street-lamp lit sidewalk through the sleet and snow.

Inside in the Fine Arts Institute on the sixth floor of the Y.W.C.A. Building, 1020 McGee Street, a merry crowd of soldiers from Camp Funston and Fort Leavenworth fox trotted and one-stepped with girls from the Fine Arts School while a sober faced young man pounded out the latest jazz music as he watched the moving figures. In a corner a private in the

56

signal corps was discussing Whistler with a black haired girl who heartily agreed with him. The private had been a member of the art colony at Chicago before the war was declared.

Three men from Funston were wandering arm in arm along the wall looking at the exhibition of paintings by Kansas City artists. The piano player stopped. The dancers clapped and cheered and he swung into "The Long, Long Trail Awinding." An infantry corporal, dancing with a swift moving girl in a red dress, bent his head close to hers and confided something about a girl in Chautauqua, Kas. In the corridor a group of girls surrounded a tow-headed young artilleryman and applauded his imitation of his pal Bill challenging the colonel, who had forgotten the password. The music stopped again and the solemn pianist rose from his stool and walked out into the hall for a drink.

A crowd of men rushed up to the girl in the red dress to plead for the next dance. Outside the woman walked along the wet lamp lit sidewalk.

It was the first dance for soldiers to be given under the auspices of the War Camp Community Service. Forty girls of the art school, chaperoned by Miss Winifred Sexton, secretary of the school and Mrs. J. F.

Binnie were the hostesses. The idea was formulated by J. P. Robertson of the War Camp Community Service, and announcements were sent to the commandants at Camp Funston and Fort Leavenworth inviting all soldiers on leave. Posters made by the girl students were put up at Leavenworth and on the interurban trains.

The first dance will be followed by others at various clubs and schools throughout the city according to Mr. Robertson.

The pianist took his seat again and the soldiers made a dash for partners. In the intermission the soldiers drank to the girls in fruit punch. The girl in red, surrounded by a crowd of men in olive drab, seated herself at the piano, the men and the girls gathered around and sang until midnight. The elevator had stopped running and so the jolly crowd bunched down the six flights of stairs and rushed waiting motor cars. After the last car had gone, the woman walked along the wet sidewalk through the sleet and looked up at the dark windows of the sixth floor.

Appendices: Possible Hemingway Stories

Assignment Sheet

The 3 January 1918 assignment sheet (see frontispiece) lists seven assignments for Hemingway: "Undertakers," "Hospitals," "General Hospital," "Union Station," "Dr. Tiffany—St. Lukes," "Jake Czhown=Gen=Shot," and "Meningitis cases."[1]

A search of the *Star* and the *Times*[2] for 3–5 January 1918 yielded three stories about Dr. Flavel B. Tiffany:

"Dr. F. B. Tiffany Near Death," *Star*, 3 January (6:30 edition), 1

"Death of Dr. F. B. Tiffany," *Star*, 4 January (6:30 edition), 1

"Dr. Flavel B. Tiffany Dead," *Times*, 5 January, 4

The last of these, an obituary, is the longest.

No stories resulting from the other six assignments have been identified. The following are noted as possibles only:

Star, 3 January

"Start Rail Pooling Here," 1

"More Freight Trains Off," 1

"Tie Up Station Approaches," 1

"City to Treat Smallpox," 1 (6:30 edition)

"Brief Bits of City News," 2 (obituaries and funerals)

"Services for Dr. E. N. La Veine," 7

Star, 4 January

"Boy Dies at School," 1

"Death of Miss Elspeth Bruce," 2

1. The only known Hemingway *Star* assignment sheet, it was donated to the Monroe County Public Library, Key West, Florida, by Mary Hemingway.

2. The *Times* was the morning sister-paper of the *Star*.

"Town Held Up For This," 2
"Yards Here in Good Shape," 10
Times, 5 January
    "Much Freight Held Up," 3
    "To Use Leeds Hospital," 3
Star, 5 January
    "Burns Kill Two in Family," 2

Fire Story

Leicester Hemingway reports these remarks by Ernest Hemingway about his *Star* apprenticeship:

> My luck was a big fire. Even the firemen were being careful. And I got inside the fire lines where I could see what was going on. It was a swell story. . . . Sparks fell all over everything. I had on a new brown suit that got burnt full of holes. After I got my information phoned in, I put down fifteen dollars on the expense account for that suit I'd ruined. But the item was turned down. It taught me a hell of a lesson. Never risk anything unless you're prepared to lose it completely—remember that. (*My Brother, Ernest Hemingway* [Cleveland: World, 1962], p. 45)

The biggest fire in Kansas City during Hemingway's time on the *Star* was the stockyards fire on 16 October. Hemingway may have phoned in material that was used in these stories in the 16 October issue:

"Set Yards Afire?" 1
"Home Guard Gathered," 2
"Plenty of Water in Mains," 2
"Two Men Saved Kansas Pens," 2
"All Fire Forces Were Out," 2

The last of these stories consisted of a series of vignettes, at least one of which has a Hemingway flavor:

> A very small boy with a very small calf stood in one of the alleyways near the fire. He had rescued the animal, he explained, and intended to keep it.

Shelling of Paris

See Theodore Brumback's account of how he and Hemingway covered the shelling of Paris (pp. 9–10). If Hemingway did cable a story to the *Star*, it has not been identified. The only possibility is "More Shells on Paris" (*Star*, 28 May 1918, 1), a very short story datelined 28 May; but since the *Chicago* sailed on 22 May, Hemingway was almost certainly not in Paris on the twenty-eighth.

Tractor Show

On Lincoln's Birthday 1918 Hemingway mentioned the Kansas City tractor show in a letter to his grandmother. It is just possible that some of the following stories were written by him:
"Tractor Show Is Ready," *Star*, 10 February 1918, 1–2
"The Tractor Is King," *Times*, 11 February 1918, 1
"The Biggest Tractor Show," *Star*, 11 February 1918, 1
"Show Types Of Plows, Also," *Star*, 11 February 1918, 3
"A Tractor Show Record," *Times*, 12 February 1918, 2
"A 'Refined' Tractor, Too," *Star*, 12 February 1918, 3
"Seeks A Big Tractor Test," *Star*, 12 February 1918, 3
"Tractors Sell Readily," *Times*, 13 February 1918, 2

Hospital Fight

On 30 January 1918 Hemingway wrote to his family that he was involved in a hospital fight and corrupt politics. Some of the following stories were probably his work:

"Pass Buck On Smallpox," *Star*, 2 January 1918, 2

"City To Treat Smallpox," *Star*, 3 January 1918, 1

"Aid For City Hospital," *Star*, 6 January 1918, 8A

"Seek Smallpox In Hotels," *Star*, 7 January 1918, 1

"Death Beat Slow Doctor," *Star*, 8 January 1918, 1

"Smallpox On The Gain," *Star*, 13 January 1918, 4A

"Plan Vaccination For All," *Star*, 21 January 1918, 1

"Carbaugh To Coon's Job," *Star*, 25 January 1918, 1

"Asks City Heads To Explain," *Star*, 25 January 1918, 1

"Health Board Quits," *Times*, 25 January 1918, 1

"Funds For New Board," *Times*, 26 January 1918, 1

"Coon May Practice Here," *Times*, 26 January 1918, 1

"Begin A Health Shakeup," *Star*, 26 January 1918, 1

"Board Has A New Problem," *Star*, 26 January 1918, 1

"Car Troubles For New Board," *Star*, 26 January 1918, 1

"Plans A Smallpox Drive," *Star*, 27 January 1918, 7A

" 'No Heed To Sick Calls,' " *Times*, 28 January 1918, 4

"To Suppress Smallpox," *Times*, 28 January 1918, 5

"Health Shakeup Goes On," *Star*, 28 January 1918, 1

"Two Health Laws Tonight," *Star*, 28 January 1918, 1

"Signs Smallpox Ordinances," *Star*, 29 January 1918, 1

"Two Health Bills Passed," *Times*, 29 January 1918, 2

"To Wipe Out Contagion," *Times*, 30 January 1918, 9

"Diseases Making Gains," *Times*, 31 January 1918, 2

"Smallpox On Kansas Side, Too," *Times*, 31 January 1918, 2

Appendix

"Tighten Up On Disease," *Star*, 31 January 1918, 4
"City Adds More Doctors," *Star*, 2 February 1918, 1
"Made A Vaccination Drive," *Star*, 3 February 1918, 1
"Vaccinated 3,733 In Drive," *Star*, 4 February 1918, 1